(UN)TETHERED

A Collection of Poems

S.V. SEGAL

Content guidance: This book includes graphic descriptions of gore and body horror that some readers might find challenging to read.

Published by River Grove Books
Austin, TX
www.rivergrovebooks.com

Copyright © 2023 S. V. Segal

All rights reserved.

Thank you for purchasing an authorized edition of this book and for complying with copyright law. No part of this book may be reproduced, stored in a retrieval system, or transmitted by any means, electronic, mechanical, photocopying, recording, or otherwise, without written permission from the copyright holder.

Distributed by River Grove Books

Design and composition by Greenleaf Book Group
Cover design by Greenleaf Book Group
Cover images: ©iStockphoto/TPopova

Publisher's Cataloging-in-Publication data is available.

Print ISBN: 978-1-63299-661-9

eBook ISBN: 978-1-63299-662-6

First Edition

To the person reading these words:
May you find solace in this book, just as I have.

CONTENTS

1	Glass Frog	49	No Face
3	Caliginous Ashes	51	Sinew
5	The Paradox	53	Bubble Snail
7	Bloody Mirrors	55	Golden Strings
11	Alcoholic	57	Footwork
13	A Thousand Origami Cranes	61	Interchange
		63	Heavy Rain
15	Moonlight	65	Bittersweet
17	Ouroboros	67	Bloodlust
19	Cotton Candy Syndrome	69	Wrath of the Lamb
21	Raw	71	Serenity (a Desk Haiku)
23	Crimson		
25	(Un)Tethered	73	Antlered Crown
31	Narcissus	75	Funambulist
33	Strangers	77	White Picket Fence
35	Rigor Mortis	79	Urge
37	Dragon King	81	Mother, Please
39	Insomnia	83	Tremors
41	Wheel of Fortune	85	Space Firefly
45	Thick as Thieves	87	Wood Frog
47	Stardust	89	Stomach Pain

91	The Deep, Dark Woods in the Middle of Nowhere	97	Vampire
		99	Honey-Tongued
93	Restless	101	Cinnamon Broom
95	Blossom	103	Midding

105	Acknowledgments
107	About the Author

GLASS FROG

If you lie on your back,
Vulnerable to wandering eyes,
Your transparent skin
Will betray the way your insides work.

How your heart rate does not match
Your mask of an expression.
The way your blood dances
In those blue veins
And how your stomach churns
Dissolves unspoken words in acid.

If you lie on your stomach,
You will blend in with the leaf below.
You will be safe from everything
That passes you by.

But just like that
You become nothing but the background
Of thousands of pictures that flash
Each time you blink the dust away.
Invisible
To predatory birds
And to the film tape
Of your memories.

Are you content
As you are?
Lonesome
And blatantly unbroken?

Cracks and fractures
Are wisdom carved in us
By the hands of suffering.

Glass was made to shatter.
And you're the most beautiful thing
That was ever created to break.

CALIGINOUS ASHES

There's an eternal flame;
Liquid fire flowing through my veins.
I spit fire to burn the rain;
I shed light time and time again.

I've flown with wings of silver hue
Across the thin veil of immortality.
I've watched roses adorn themselves with drops of dew;
I've seen both sides of human morality.

What else are we
Apart from the heartening Melpomene
And the unnerving Thalia
Intertwining irrevocably?

I've watched thousands rise and fall;
I am the hyperbole of halcyon.
The blandiloquent chiaroscuro of life;
A beatific smile carved with a knife.

My mind, fugacious and adroit,
Adumbrates to the gambol of my heartbeat.
The efflorescence peculiarity of a penumbra;
The surreptitious, mellifluous, anesthetic rhapsody.

How many times do I have to die
To numb this vicious flame?
How many wings do I have to cut
To see the sun again?

THE PARADOX

A bubbly cynic with nihilistic optimism
Paints life with dead dreams
And rises again from something
To become nothing

BLOODY MIRRORS

Hands curl around the edges of a sink.
Is it cold, or are the hands frozen?
Shut tight with white knuckles,
Hold on to anything as long as it doesn't break.

A tilt of the neck,
A thundering crackle of painful lightning,
Tense movement under smooth marble.

Sickly skin against vivid veins.
Sluggish crimson rivers
Desperate to see tomorrow
Even though they can't see today.

Windows of the soul,
Black satin curtains,
Speckled with red ink,
Bleed roads inside a map.

A tug of war between illusion and delusion,
A slithering rope coiled, a choker,
Embedded with rubies and sapphires.

Ignore the bruises, they will go away.
What won't leave is the cracking marble,
The narrowing bloodshot eyes,
The lips that curl into an attempted smile,
An attempted murder against the self.

Swing broken bones and find broken glass;
Shatter the reflection that stared back.

Dead but not buried.
The abyss finds a way to crawl back without legs,
To stare without eyes,
To laugh without voice.

It settles itself in the crook of the ribs,
Pounding against flesh.
Maybe it was preferable to keep the mirror;
Now, there's no walking away.

But now that you're familiar,
You uncurl your fists
And speak with a soft voice
As to not scare it.
As to not scare yourself.
You sing when it screams,
You thrive when it sleeps,
You sigh when it wakes up to say hello again.

You want to learn how to hold hands,
How to float between stars,
And wave across a train station goodbye.
But instead, you learn how to breathe smoke and cough dead constellations,
How to dance across lifelines and speed limits,

How to ignore the angry birds that peck your face to watch you bleed,
How to hold the void with tender arms and rock it to sleep.
You can be one together
And invite life to come your way.

ALCOHOLIC

Like an alcoholic
Even the very sight
Triggers the poison.
Do you feel like throwing up too?

Chest becomes heavy,
Palpitations rattle the ribs.
Not sad,
Just empty.

Used to be milk and honey.
Now just a dark cloud
On a stormy night
Casting lightning cracks
On dry skin.

I hope you feel like throwing up too.

A THOUSAND ORIGAMI CRANES

Haven't showered in days.
I see no point.
Can't cleanse
The mudslide slugging
Through my veins.

If being happy is a sin,
Then call me holy
Cuz I ain't got no devil in me.
I got nothing in me.

Paper cranes fly toward the sun.
They want to be free but burn before they get home.
At least they grant wishes along the way.

Sailing purposelessly in an ocean
Made of ink and black holes.
Folding paper ceaselessly
And staying away from the edges of the boat.

Got the Candyman on speed dial,
But he gives me no sugar.
I need to snort salt
To keep the demons at bay.

The loudest silence
Is in a hospital's waiting room.
Everyone asks themselves:
"What happens now?"

Hands cramped from hopeful origami,
I fold another crane's wing.
The answer is always the same:
"I don't know."

MOONLIGHT

Without the sun,
I shrivel in heaps of dark despair.
I need it to survive.
Humans are dependent,
And I take it for granted.

I exist in gray shades
Of fleeting sunshine,
Of fleeting darkness,
With a pair of sockets
That have colorblind prism irises.

Like a broken compass
There is no direction
Or destination.
There is just floating
In endless space and time.

But now,
Moonlight breaks through,
Your midnight sun
Piercing the hollow abyss.
Illuminating a woven path
Across the ragged trees.

I am lost,
And I choose not to be found.

I am lost,
And as long as I'm lost with you,
I will find some way
To make this vessel stay.

You're my moonlight,
And I will drift peacefully
Across galaxies and oceans
To make it as far as tomorrow.

OUROBOROS

I am infinite
And whole
And ethereal

With gnashing teeth
I consume myself
Over and over again.

I taste my thick blood
And use it to wash down
My godly remains.

I kill myself,
Then bring myself
Back to life.
I am my own creator.

I choose to destroy
Identity,
Along with perception,
I become nothing
And everything at once
Becomes meaningless.

So, when you see me
In the back of your eyelids,
Facing the Angel of Death

I am crashing into myself
Like meeting a familiar stranger
In an abandoned grocery aisle.

And my smile will be bloody
With crooked and jagged teeth.
You'll recognize the cycle
Because all I've ever done
Is make myself
Infinite, whole, and ethereal.

Consumed.
Over and over
And over
Again.

COTTON CANDY SYNDROME

There's a carnival in town with big neon signs.
Sugary highs and adrenaline spikes
Give birth to laughing children.

There's palpable electricity in the humid air
That drenches the crowd
In a thrilling euphoria.

Clowns make grown people cry
And scream in the rawness of childhood.
The authenticity of freedom.

Laughter can sound so similar
To hysterical sobbing.
Sometimes it's hard to tell, since it's all chemicals anyway.

Don't be scared if you're not like the rest.
If rollercoasters don't make you feel alive
Because nothing else really does.

Or if the haunted house doesn't scare
The life left out of you.
Don't be scared if all you have left

Is the moment you place the cotton candy
In your tasteless mouth
And for one moment, you taste the sweet relief of something

Tangible.
But just as it came,
It is gone.

Fleeting like the wind that whips
Your hair to cover your eyes.
And now your mouth tastes more like blood.

Your chemicals died
On your tongue.
At least it tastes like something again.

When you start drooling
Pink from your mouth,
Don't wipe it off.

Only the universe knows when you'll taste again.

RAW

Promises of a new tomorrow
Hang in the broken past.
A rope of unspoken words
And harsh truths, coiling,
Suffocating life from a sore throat.
Collapsing airways.

Ice and stone, sharp and hardened,
Glinting with crimson pools.
Calloused hearts viscerally
Crashing against bone cages.

Next to the water,
Swinging and laughing,
Are the songs of nightingales.
Clinging to salt water and sunsets,
Sounds of hope rattling their lungs,
Starlit eyes smiling.

Next to the water,
Deep blue waves crashing
Ideals of human gods.
Mortal minds sneering
At immortal souls.

The dust settles,
And the nightingales sing their final song.

CRIMSON

Blood is considered
Frightening.
Blood, a sign of death,
Barrels toward you like life.
Snatches everything vital
Before you've even blinked twice.

Lifeblood taints the skin
With unspoken secrets
Of past horrors.
Don't speak or you lose your voice.

But some consider it beautiful,
A life force
That binds us together
And launches us into existence.

Blood is life when rosy cheeks shine
In embarrassment or when
It rushes like wild rivers,
Taking adrenaline as a passenger, when

Your heart is about to burst
From your chest and your blood
Sings loudly in your ears.
Listen.

Pay attention.
Bleed yourself into life
In the way you know best.
Stay up with bloodshot eyes
With your insomniac friend.

Or hang upside down
From the monkey bars
Of your old elementary school
And watch your life flash before your eyes
Once again.

Merge life and death together
As you walk into the meadow of hope.
Rest your body among the wildflowers
And bleed yourself into the earth.

It has been waiting for you
For a long, long time.

(UN)TETHERED

You always thought you wore
Various rings because aesthetically
It was pretty.
Which it is.

But you became aware of how
Solid it felt
To clench your fist and have metal
Bite into you
With a sort of uncomfortable intimacy
You couldn't get any other way.

It seems natural
To stick pins in your hands
When you're bored.
Feeling a sting that pulsates
And threatens to implode your skin.

The blade is familiar,
And so is the Emptiness
That drowns your heart.
And in those peculiar moments,
You are life and death, combined.
Your soul,
Like a wandering jellyfish,
Swimming into the darkness,

Loses itself and becomes one
With the ocean.

Purple rings
In your stomach.
Home to stillborn
Dreams.

There is beauty in losing yourself
To the depths.
You recognize yourself in the darkness
When the light can't hurt your eyes.

There is no fear.
Just questions that dart around,
Swimming past you as you
Wander deeper,
Like frightened fish that need sunlight
To breathe.

You think you hear garbled voices
Screaming at you from the surface.
Sounds akin to your name.

But you have long forgotten
Useless information
And many other things
That you cannot even name.

They are like the food
You consume:
Tasteless and unnecessary.

Your scrambled words
Are the resulting vomit
Of trespassed boundaries
That crush the wandering spirit
Left in you.

Your murky word vomit
Is hard to decipher
But small chunks cling to your ligaments.
They feel familiar.
Like getting strep throat
For the third year in a row.

You are an odd creature
Of a curious nature.
With three eyes and numb nerves,
A dormant heart and a muddled brain,
That can't seem to make
A full human being.

The deeper you swim,
The more content you become.
You lose your vision and you wonder
If you've gone blind or if the world

Is too bright for eyes like yours.
It doesn't matter anyway.
None of it does.
Closing your eyes is like falling asleep
For the last time.
Breathing sounds like a flat line
In reverse.
One way or another,
What difference does it make?

You are content with the universe
And yourself,
Believe it or not.
There is just a bone-deep tiredness that
Hugs your skeleton
And sways your opinion.
How long do you want to put up
With one side of the coin before you flip
To the other?

There is not much there,
In that jellyfish soul of yours.
But there is a twinge of relief
That comes with indifference
Because when the darkness settles
In your rib cage,
It is just as familiar as the sun rays
That dance on your skin.

You keep floating,
Wandering and wondering aimlessly
Like a dead star long gone cold.
Quietly you sing to keep yourself
Company.

When untethering yourself
Is the same as being tethered,
You are at peace with yourself.

And that is the one thing that matters.

NARCISSUS

How peculiar is it
That when you stare into my eyes,
You only see your reflection.

As if I were a river
That solely existed
To show you exactly
What you wanted.

It takes two to tango
And two to have a dialogue,
But you're stuck in soliloquy,
And I've already exited the stage.

I'm done playing pretend
Along the riverbank
Where the daffodils grow.

Turns out, you were right,
I am a river.
I glide gently in this world
Among many other tumultuous
Bodies of water.
While others are the thrashing seas
Or the freezing rain,
I am quiet and omniscient.

Whether you stay
Along my riverside
Or you wilt and turn gray
Doesn't really matter.

A river never stops for a flower.

STRANGERS

You tell me that the back-and-forth,
The seesaw of doubt,
Hurts.

I can't feel anything
As you tell me that this is the last straw—
My choice to continue the blood flow
That runs between our veins.

I wonder, as you hang up,
If we miss strangers once they're gone
Because we thought we knew them
When they stood by our side.

But I never knew you.
At least not well enough to understand
Why you did the things you proclaimed
Were in the name of love.

Like the ocean where you grew up,
You look beautiful from the sand.
But the water is bone-chilling
Once you step in it.

RIGOR MORTIS

How peculiar is it
That only when blood runs cold
Do warm words grace the ears.

When the muscles harden,
The death grip of the living
Ignites the flame of the dead's memories
Into a wildfire.

The seeds that were meant to be trees
Sprouted into white lilies that now lie
Atop the ashes that for only a moment
Burned as embers.

If we loved the living
The way we loved the dead,
The dark would just be evening,
The earth simply a bed.

DRAGON KING

You said you couldn't live like a dog
Because you were born to be a tiger.
But those are the words of a dragon
That hasn't yet looked into the river.

Four-toed beast with jagged teeth,
Tongue as sharp as the blades that tried
To impale themselves into your scales;
Eighty-one if you count with your third eye.

Your lesser brethren, the snakes, bare their fangs,
Their envious venom clouding their vision.
A mutt with scales masquerading as a reptile
Is all they make you out to be.

Knee-deep in river water,
They expect you to be docile,
Which, of course, you are
But not to them.

Smoke rises from your nostrils
As you spit fire from your lungs.
Villagers with star-struck eyes
Wish their inner flame wasn't victim to the wind.

But that's what dragons do.
They start a wildfire across nations

And light the way for those
Who are afraid of the dark.

The crown weighs heavy.
Rest your weary eyes
As you sit on a throne of your blood,
Sweat and tears.

At the top of the world
Your dreams tend to lie at your feet.
But if you look up,
The stars have never been more beautiful.

INSOMNIA

Waiting for you is
Dizzying despair
That tastes like bitter coffee.

Waiting for you is
A myriad of dreams
That belong to the day
When they should belong
To the dark sea that swims
Behind one's eyes.

Waiting for you is
Nothing and everything
In a world that falls asleep at your feet,
Begging to let go of nightmares.

Waiting for you is
Looking out of a window
And waiting for someone
Who will never come home.

WHEEL OF FORTUNE

Oh, ticking hand,
Where do you land?
Is it red?
The sound of slammed doors,
Clenched fists and churning bile,
Words that claw into your heart
Like ravenous parasites bursting a vein.
Bones on asphalt and tears
That can't wipe away the blood
Falling from your nose.

Oh, ticking hand,
Where do you land?
Is it yellow?
Giggles and flushed cheeks.
Skipping somewhere because walking
Doesn't do your butterflies justice.
Spilling yourself on paper and watching
Flowers with no name bloom for no reason.

Oh, ticking hand,
Where do you land?
Is it orange?
Bouncing your leg faster
Than the racing thoughts that jumble
And turn your stomach

Into a bottomless canyon of obscure possibilities.
The dark envelops and you curl
Tightly into yourself like a child
In a forest, lost.

Oh, ticking hand,
Where do you land?
Is it green?
Getting to the top of the mountain
After crawling for so long.
You can touch the sky
With those fingertips of yours.
The clouds are your kingdom.
You won't fall because you were born ethereal
And made of everything that tried to break you.
Pluck a piece of fluffy white cotton candy,
And it will turn your tongue gold.
Nothing could taste better
Than crossing the finish line.

Oh, ticking hand,
Where do you land?
Is it blue?
Floating among stars as you watch
The world fall asleep to see tomorrow.
Rain gliding down a window as the moon
Follows your car on the way home.
You dream of being held

By the earth that created you
As you're rocked and sung a lullaby by beings
You've never met.
Everything makes sense to you
For the first time.

Oh, ticking hand,
Where do you land?
Is it pink?
Food that tastes like medicine,
Silent footsteps that echo in the dark.
You've lived with your eyes closed
For so long that maps live behind
Your eyelids.
A hole so deep and dark,
Who dared to reach into your heart
And rip you into pieces;
Stop picking at the scab.
It'll leave a scar.
Salt water carves your cheeks
Into vices of your ancestors
Who tried to fill their abyss
Just like you.

Oh, ticking hand,
Does it matter where you land?
The world scraped its knees and bled itself
Into primordial chaos.

The colors of your wheel are watercolor paint
That the flood washed away long ago.
The ticking hand is now sand in an hourglass
Opening a new door
When yours finally closes.

THICK AS THIEVES

When we meet,
Shall we meet as strangers?
Glancing at each other
With curiosity and sympathy.
Letting me lean on you
Because my leg aches
From kicking the bucket too hard.
You hiding
Your ghost of a smile;
First-timers always get it wrong.

Will we be acquaintances?
You'll place your hands on mine,
Helping me push up daisies
And watching them bloom.
I'll get you a bouquet of forget-me-nots
So you'll be able to pick my atoms
From out of the multitude.

Will we be old friends
Who have danced this tango
For so long
That we recognize each other
In the eyes of others
And have mastered the art of
Evanescent belonging?

Ephemeral obscurity,
An oblivion of immortality-challenged
Who stare at the night sky
And wonder when they'll meet you,
What you'll look like,
And if you'll be kind to them.

Time always goes by faster
When it's running out.
But if you welcome me
With open arms,
I'll run to you, old friend.

STARDUST

When we go back
To our primordial soup,
It'll taste like garlic bread
And yerba mate on a lazy Sunday.

Our stars will be so close
We could hold hands
And laugh at people
Who push a pull door
Or get shit on by a bird.

Our atoms are so interlaced
We are a dying core going cold
Or a black hole being born.

My precious, shining, little star,
I'll never have to wonder
Who you are
Because we knew each other
When we were flesh
And we've gone back
To what we always were:
Stardust.
No more, no less.

NO FACE

So many expressions:
Glittering eyes and clenched teeth,
Crinkled victorious grins
In the corners of their eyes.
Origami paper folded
Into inalienable countenance.

They, with their many imposed expressions, claw out
The Someone, the Anyone,
Who by any name
Could only exist as themselves
Under the surface.

Myriad of hands edge closer
To flick brushstrokes
On the empty canvas of a face.

A rose by another name
Would still carve your flesh
With thorns.
Just like a rose
With any other face
Would live a thousand lives,
Then irrevocably wilt.

Check the reflection once,
And make sure
To check it twice.

Your face
Is no face
Just out of sight.

SINEW

Blood born
Out of soldier cells;
I am small.
Bridge
Between muscle and bone.

You can't replace me,
Gorilla glue.
I am limbo,
And you have not gone low enough
To get past me.

Burn me as you cross me,
For dancing on brimstone barefoot
Is a sign of respect,
And I will not tolerate you
Stepping on me
Without leaving the consequences singed
On your sole.

BUBBLE SNAIL

Obsidian beady eyes
Watching from the beginning.
Curious antennae twitching
As a new body curls
Into itself.
Molding itself to face
The outside.
Naïve and hopeful
Cell courage.

I'll pick you up
And kiss your bubble
For good luck.
I know what it's like
To be slower than the rest.
Worry not;
There is no finish line.

Sweet, little Bubble Snail,
Pop into earth anew,
And children will admire you,
As I once did,
On the way to school.

GOLDEN STRINGS

A door creaks in a hallway.
I close my eyes and suddenly
I'm on a wooden bench
In front of a piano,
And you're in the living room.
Midas with a violin,
Plucking people's souls
Until they collapsed into gold.
Your love is as holy
As your rage is petrifying.
You've burned holes with each step
In a world that considered compassion
A weakness.

Our story is a rollercoaster
Of madness,
And when I get vertigo,
You scream profanities
About getting on the ride.

Whether you believe in fate
Or architecture,
We are intertwined
Since womb immemorial.
Let's play a tune immortal;
I'll dance on silver keys.
A sempiternal song
You'll sing with golden strings.

FOOTWORK

These feet
Were made for dancing
Under purple lightning
And freezing rain
In the middle of a meadow
Of wildflowers

If we step on each other
We'll just laugh
And keep singing
Until our voices
Grow hoarse

These feet
Were made to spar
And wound each other
Like true warriors
Who have something to lose
And our blood will taste the same
Under the moonlight

These feet
Were made to walk as far
As the midway point
Where they'll wait for your feet
To synchronize pace and together we will see
Where this journey leads

These feet
Were not made for chasing
And if you turn and walk away
I will plant myself
Where I stand
And bloom flowers that smell
Like funeral dirt
And missed train stops

These feet
Will make a home
Where they've always stood
Resilient to the wind
Growing steadier after all these years

These feet
Will not kick
Like a frightened horse
Or an angry emu
At those who have caused
Blisters and calluses

These feet
Will wait for your feet
To retrace the footsteps
Back to the midway point

If you're brave enough
We can learn how to dance together
Under the stars again
And if not

These feet
Will bandage themselves
And keep on walking
Down a winding road of gray
And learn more footwork
Along the way

INTERCHANGE

Sitting in a white chair
In front of a screen full
Of poets watching poets
Speak about the immortality
Of words and the search
For answers, which guide
Our writing and human experience.
The door opens,
Boisterous like your affection.
Love monster with a drink
Clutched in your claws.
My eyes widen.
Your smile is enormous
Like the size of the sugary
Glass that sloshes
Ginger brown liquid and persimmon.
Your lips graze my forehead repeatedly,
And I let you
Because your love language is
Giving everything including yourself
And my love language is
letting my physical form
Tolerate tangible existence
For a particular moment.
Because your kisses
Are one of my favorite

Forms of uncomfortable reminder
That compromise and exchange
Are the currency of love.

HEAVY RAIN

It floods like tears of a god who lost everything
Because people no longer have faith.
It floods like a dam broke upstream,
Violent, powerful, sweeping, drowning
Everything in its path like a chip
On your shoulder that shattered
and bled into the cracks
Of the pavement and tainted the soles
Of strangers' feet.
It floods like unwanted bile
In the tiles of your clenched teeth.
It floods like the sweat of your people
When they suffer in the heat
Of an unforgiving sun
Because the AC doesn't work,
And no one gives a fuck
About fixing it.
It floods like salt water
Into the wounds in your arms;
You have no idea how they got there,
You swear.
It floods around you
and people you've never met,
But somehow we're all walking through the flood

Soaked, shivering, tired, determined
To make our way home.

BITTERSWEET

In the candy aisle
Of the local shop,
Rows of chocolates
Wait and watch
For a poor soul
To pick them up.

What is it now?
Whose trembling fingers
Will be tainted
With delicious regret?

A guilt so dark and deep
Even Willy Wonka refuses
To gnaw on the molten,
Rotten, cocoa taste
Of apology.

May the ravenous river
Of this undoing
Drown their lungs
In Hershey kisses.

BLOODLUST

Fear paints your pupils
Wider and darker
With each stroke of
The dancing blade
Carving my sadistic intention
Into your desperate flesh.

My name is the only prayer
That taints your sinning tongue,
But no amount of pleading
Will save you from salvation.

Your voice was meant
For begging.
Confess how much
You want to live
As my hand curls like a viper
Around your pulsing throat
And my teeth sink into you,
Drowning in your taste
And delivering you the poison
That you can't decide if you really want.

Your whispers of gratitude
Turn into implorations for mercy.
My teeth bare as I laugh;
I never learned to speak French,
And I won't start now.

You and I are victims
Of each other's passions,
And I crave to mark my territory
On your bloody grave.

But first I'll take my time
To enjoy the way your screams
Ring in my ears.
And the way our intimate,
Violent dance
Drags us both
Into feral oblivion.

WRATH OF THE LAMB

I have never met you,
But my clay was molded
By whatever god you believe in
To hold your hands delicately
When the feathered raven stag
Jolts you from sleep and causes
Your breath to hyperventilate
On a cold, lonely night.

I am no one to you,
But I know your name
And the way you smell
Like a boat sailing on salt water.
The way you hate eyes
And their tumultuous depths.
How your mind creates forts
Because the inside of your mind palace
Is haunted by ghosts you fear to name.

Sharing a meal with me
Is not a mind game.
My words are the glass
That cut through the dark,
And the recipe I use
Is from a mother who loved me
When the world collapsed on her.

Despite the Cabernet Sauvignon in her blood,
Fructose granules clung to my cheek
When she kissed it.
She never tried to make her misery
My own.

Who knows if our stories will change
If we try and yank our legs
From this obsidian wolf trap.
All I know is this is your design,
And all I want
Is to show you mine.

SERENITY
(A DESK HAIKU)

flowers bloom in lungs
vines sew up wounds cracked through cement
the earth rejoices

ANTLERED CROWN

The arrogant hunger
And senseless violence
Are dishonorable reasons
For indulging the feral beast
Who bares its teeth seeking blood.

You were created
Indomitable.
And yet judgment comes for us all.

When your heart is heavier
Than the feather,
Remember that your god
Is cruel
Because you willed him to be.

FUNAMBULIST

I extend my shaking hand
Toward you
As you climb onto the ledge,
Turning and laughing
At the wideness of my eyes.

"The wind is perfect,"
You say.
You have a strong
Set of shoulders to carry that stubborn
Head of yours.

You've done this all before, apparently,
But I am like the rope
The wind pushes around
Unsteady at your feet.

When the rope buckles,
We both understand
It wasn't you I didn't trust.

The wind howls,
Burning our throats.
Sometimes all you can do
When there's a misstep
Is give in to the fall.

WHITE PICKET FENCE

My blood paints over the ivory wooden bones
That shred my skin like paper.

Your white paper face
Crumples in disapproval

Watches as I haul and howl
Over the fence to my escape

And leave a trail of my insides,
A path you seek to follow.

I slump into the ground,
And you say that freedom

Will cost me everything.
I laugh as you walk away

Further into your ivory cage.
I bleed into the wildflowers.

Who knew that freedom
Tasted so metallic.

URGE

Don't take this
The wrong way,
But I want your blood
So far deep under
My fingernails
Everyone knows
I am responsible
For your unbecoming.

Your flesh
Is stuck between my teeth,
And I let it
Rot my breath
So when I speak,
You are the undercurrent
That pulls experienced swimmers
To ancient sunken cities.

You tremble
In my presence
Because once I stood
At the edge of your bed
Holding a knife.
And to this day
I can't tell
If I was dreaming.

You know I am capable
Of visceral evisceration.

I sing to you
Until the sun
Gives up on us
And the moon
Sighs and finally looks away.

MOTHER, PLEASE

We can admire
Your favorite stars

The Three Marias.

Your eyes shine
Just like them.

My bones are heavy,
I say,
But you tell me
I'm just a lotus flower
That was born
From too much mud.

I'm tired
In the way we think stars still shine
Long after they've died
Out alone
In the darkness of space.

Mother, please,
You've carried me for so long.
What's a little more?
The grave is like your womb
And as you let go,
The Earth is your arms
Enveloping me.

TREMORS

My hands are unsteady,
My dear.
But I never waver
In the face of fear.
Failure will drive me
To be braver for those
Who are afraid to lose me.

The fearless are cowards
With nothing to lose.
I guess I am a coward then
Who will go to war
With my brain and my throat
In my hands.

We are all unsteady,
My darling.
My mother had heart tremors
For eight years,
But her hands
Could raise mountains
And her voice, the nightingales
That sang by the water.

Your voice shakes
When the fortress of your mind
Crumbles into ashes

And the world seems
To be an earthquake.

But your hands are steady,
And we become two shaky halves
Of a steady whole.

SPACE FIREFLY

I didn't remember you
For so long.
But last night,
I dreamed that you could fly
And you showed me
The sea from the sky.
I remembered your soft words
And your galaxy eyes,
And I knew
That if I fell, you would catch me
Before I hit the water.
You know what shattering feels like,
And you can't bear pain
In others that is just like your own.

I cannot fly,
But I can pick up pieces,
No matter how broken.
I am used to bleeding hands.
To hold you
Is catching a firefly
In a jar,
Setting it free,
And realizing
That it's actually a star
That is very far from home.

WOOD FROG

When winter comes
And you're left out
In the cold, white snow,
Your blood will freeze
And your heart
Will stop beating.

You'll feel dead,
But you're just waiting
To wake up
From the hibernation
That heals the frostbite
That turned you blue.

When the April sunrays
Dance on your skin
And kiss it gold,
Your heart will be reborn
And your eyes
Will bloom open.
It's time to live again
Until next winter.
When the first snowflake
Rains from the sky,
You feel your heartbeat
Slow down.

Your eyes will shut
And you'll think to yourself
How much warmer
Winter seems to be
This time around.

STOMACH PAIN

"This is different."
I can't say much more
As I vomit into the toilet bowl.

"What makes it different?"
You ask.

Usually, my stomach hurts
Because I've eaten too much
Or the ulcers I think I have
Coat my stomach like paint.

It lasts for hours sometimes,
And I can't sleep.
I sweat and curse and pace
And wonder what it takes
To make the pain go away.

I'll eat better
And make my portions smaller,
But the pain comes anyway.
I'll go to the doctor soon.

"So what is this then?"
You ask.
"How is this different?"

I laugh.
"This is betrayal."
It feels like poisonous lead in my gut
Because I knew something was wrong
And it hurts to be proven right.

It's not my fault for being blindsided.
And yet
I want to rip out my eyes.

"There is no medicine for this,"
I say as my repressed emotions
Play jump rope with my intestines.
Time will sew the stitches
Someone else has caused.

But for now,
The toilet seat is cold against my cheek,
And I just want to be able to eat again
Without being afraid.

THE DEEP, DARK WOODS IN THE MIDDLE OF NOWHERE

If you walk barefooted across the fields
Of lonely grass,
The trees will watch and pray
That you don't trip on their roots
But find your way
Back to yourself.

If you scream or cry,
The wind will carry your voice
To your own ears
So you can hear yourself
For the first time,
Almost like someone else
Begging for help and love
That has long been overdue.

And if with your withered hands
You dig your own grave
And lay to rest,
You will wake up in your bed
With dirt under your nails
And a sore throat,
The trees gently tapping
At your window

To remind you
That the sun will come up soon
And you can always try
To listen again.

Don't keep yourself waiting.

RESTLESS

Deep in my stomach
I feel you,
My child.

You grow and grow
And wait to be born.

And when I hold you back
In fear of greatness or neglect,
You spread and wound yourself
Tighter inside me.

I cannot breathe
Or move
Without the pain of your existence
Haunting me
And reminding me
That your birth
Is inevitable.

The things we have been born to create,
If left inside of us where they do not belong,
Will fester and rot in ways
That only the things we love
Manage to do.
My child, be patient,
The first birth is always the hardest.

BLOSSOM

We are small and insignificant
In the grand scheme of things.
Still, we can be as big
As we let ourselves grow.

Sprouting little buds
That want to be important
And look up at the stars.
No wonder:
We're made up of the same things.

How terrifying for a seed
To realize that we can all be giants.

VAMPIRE

You bit me,
And when you lost your tooth,
You blamed me.

I guess self-awareness
Is for people with canines
Instead of fangs.

HONEY-TONGUED

Your words cloy my taste buds
To a bitter end.

Sweet, so sweet,
I wonder why you want so many bees.

The honey might reach your throat,
But it will never reach
Your heart.

CINNAMON BROOM

Time to sweep the floor
And sweep, sweep, sweep
Everything out the door.

The footprints of ghosts,
The dust on books,
The dried blood of wounds
That don't bleed anymore.

Such a tiring chore.

When you're done,
Your muscles will ache,
And you'll wonder if it's worth it
To get rid of everything.

But you'll realize that breathing
And dancing are so much easier
When you make your space
Your own.

MIDDING

Sitting at the edge of a campfire,
The glow of light colors me like sunset,
And my cold drink numbs my hand.

Alone at the edge
While everyone else's voices
Ebb and flow like a river
I've dipped my feet in.

Alone at the edge . . . of what?
A mental precipice that watches the painting
Etch itself along the canvas.

This warm contentment
Of belonging without participating,
Taking a step back as everyone keeps walking,
Listening to off-key singing
As I rest my head against the car window.

Everything I have and will ever have
Is not guaranteed
Except in the very moment
That I have it.

Worrying about it
Means I have nothing,

Even if it's in front of me,
And I refuse to miss things
That have not yet gone.

I let the fire warm my hands
And my smile.
In the eyes of presence
And at the edge of belonging
Is where I let go.

ACKNOWLEDGMENTS

Publishing a book is like raising a child. It takes a village.

To my team at Greenleaf: Thank you for taking a chance on me. The birthing process was gentler with you holding my hand.

To my loved ones: You are my muses and the wind beneath my wings. This book is yours just as much as it is mine.

To myself: I am eternally grateful that you clung to this dream that meant so much to you. Couldn't have done it without you.

ABOUT THE AUTHOR

S. V. SEGAL grew up wandering the aisles of bookstores wishing to see their own writing on the shelves someday. Now that this book has fulfilled this dream, they request that each reader who comes upon this book join their loyal army of mischievous henchmen. Health benefits and spiritual enlightenment included.

www.ingramcontent.com/pod-product-compliance
Lightning Source LLC
Chambersburg PA
CBHW030506080526
44586CB00029B/728